Bird Brains

JEREMY HYMAN, PhD

ILLUSTRATED BY HAUDE LEVESQUE, PhD

Bird Brains

THE WILD & WACKY WORLD OF BIRDS

JEREMY HYMAN, PhD

ILLUSTRATED BY
HAUDE
LEVESQUE, PhD

MoonDance

Quarto is the authority on a wide range of topics.
Quarto educates, entertains, and enriches the lives of our readers—
enthusiasts and lovers of hands-on living.
www.quartoknows.com

Produced by EarlyLight Books
Page Layout: Dawn Cusick
Proofreading: Meredith Hale

6 Orchard Road, Suite 100
Lake Forest, CA 92630
quartoknows.com
Visit our blogs at quartoknows.com

Printed in China
1 3 5 7 9 10 8 6 4 2

— *To my Grandpa,*
who shared his love of birds with me

Contents

Great Adaptations 47

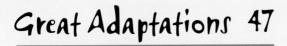

Introduction

Welcome to the amazing world of birds! Around the globe, there are about ten thousand bird species. Birds can be found in almost every habitat, from mountains and forests to deserts and the open ocean. They range in size from giant, flightless ostriches, to soaring albatrosses, to tiny, buzzing hummingbirds.

There are birds that sip nectar from flowers, birds that eat fruit, and birds that eat seeds. There are birds that eat insects, birds that eat meat, and birds that eat other birds and bird eggs. Birds come in colors from black as night, to white as snow, to every color of the rainbow. There are birds that sing, of course, but also birds that grunt, hiss, and quack.

We may appreciate birds most for their colorful feathers and beautiful songs, but they also have amazing brains. When you're watching birds, it's fun to wonder what's going on in their heads. Birds are smarter than we might realize. They know a lot about the world around them, and some of them even use new tools and skills to solve problems. We have learned so much about their lives. Who knows what we might learn next!

Jeremy Hyman

Meet the Birds

What Is a Bird?

Birds are vertebrates, which means that they have a backbone and a skull. Fish, reptiles, amphibians, and mammals are also vertebrates. Much of what sets birds apart may have been shaped by the demands of flight. Their front limbs have become wings, and the broad surfaces of their wings are covered with feathers, the most unique bird trait.

All modern birds have wings and feathers. Even birds that cannot fly, such as penguins, kiwis, emus, and ostriches, have wings and feathers. A North Island brown kiwi's wings are so small that you can hardly see them underneath its shaggy coat of feathers!

Some birds, such as common eiders and tree swallows, line their nests with soft down feathers to help keep their eggs and nestlings warm. Feathers help birds to be camouflaged in their habitats, whether they are rock wrens, hiding in boulders and gravel, or yellow-naped Amazon parrots, blending into their green forest homes. Bird feathers also come in every color of the rainbow, especially when feathers are used for display to attract mates or to repel rivals. Some of the biggest and most spectacular feathers, plumes of a King of Saxony bird of paradise or the tail feathers of a long-tailed widowbird, are clearly for display. In fact, the size of those feathers probably makes it harder for those birds to fly.

The feathers found on the wings and tails of most birds are stiff and strong. These feathers are used for flight.

Not all feathers are for flight. Birds also have contour feathers covering their bodies. These feathers work to streamline and waterproof them.

Underneath the contour feathers, downy feathers serve as insulation.

Bird Biologists

Scientists who study birds are called ornithologists. Some ornithologists study topics such as bird evolution. They work to understand how birds evolved from reptiles, or how modern birds are related to one another. Other ornithologists study bird anatomy to learn how birds fly, how feathers grow, or how bird lungs or eyes work. And other ornithologists study bird behavior, working to understand how much birds know about the world around them, such as where to find food and shelter.

Birds have complex social lives. They know a lot about their neighbors and flock mates, and they have the ability to communicate with those around them. Birds are smarter than we might realize, and they have amazing brains.

But what makes an amazing brain? Some scientists think that birds' big brains may have evolved because flying is a tricky business. Measuring intelligence is challenging, especially in wild animals, but it's fair to say that all birds are smart enough to solve the common problems in their lives.

The largest bird brain belongs to the largest bird, the ostrich. But the ostrich's brain is not big compared to its body size. Other birds have bigger brains for their size, such as crows, parrots, songbirds, and herons, and these are the groups of birds that are known for being clever problem solvers and tool users.

(Check out pages 58 through 67 to learn more about these birds.)

Bird Anatomy

Besides feathers, birds have other adaptations that help them fly. They have lightweight skeletons with hollow bones, which makes it easier for them to fly. Birds also have toothless beaks instead of jaws full of teeth, and short tails that end in a set of fused vertebrae called the pygostyle. Even birds with long tails have short skeletons, and their long tail feathers are attached to their skeletons.

Most birds also have a large keel on the sternum where their big flight muscles are attached. It takes a lot of muscle to get off the ground and fly! Penguins have big keels because they need big muscles to fly through the water, but kiwis, emus, and ostriches have flat sternums.

The modern birds we see today are not the only kinds of birds that have ever lived. Millions of years ago, birds such as the archaeopteryx had bird-like traits such as wings and feathers, but also reptile-like traits such as teeth and long, bony tails. Other traits, such as scales on their legs and laying eggs, are shared by both birds and reptiles.

The differences between birds and reptiles might seem obvious today, but if you went bird-watching 150 million years ago, you might have seen some toothy birds and feathered reptiles that would have made the line between birds and reptiles a little fuzzier!

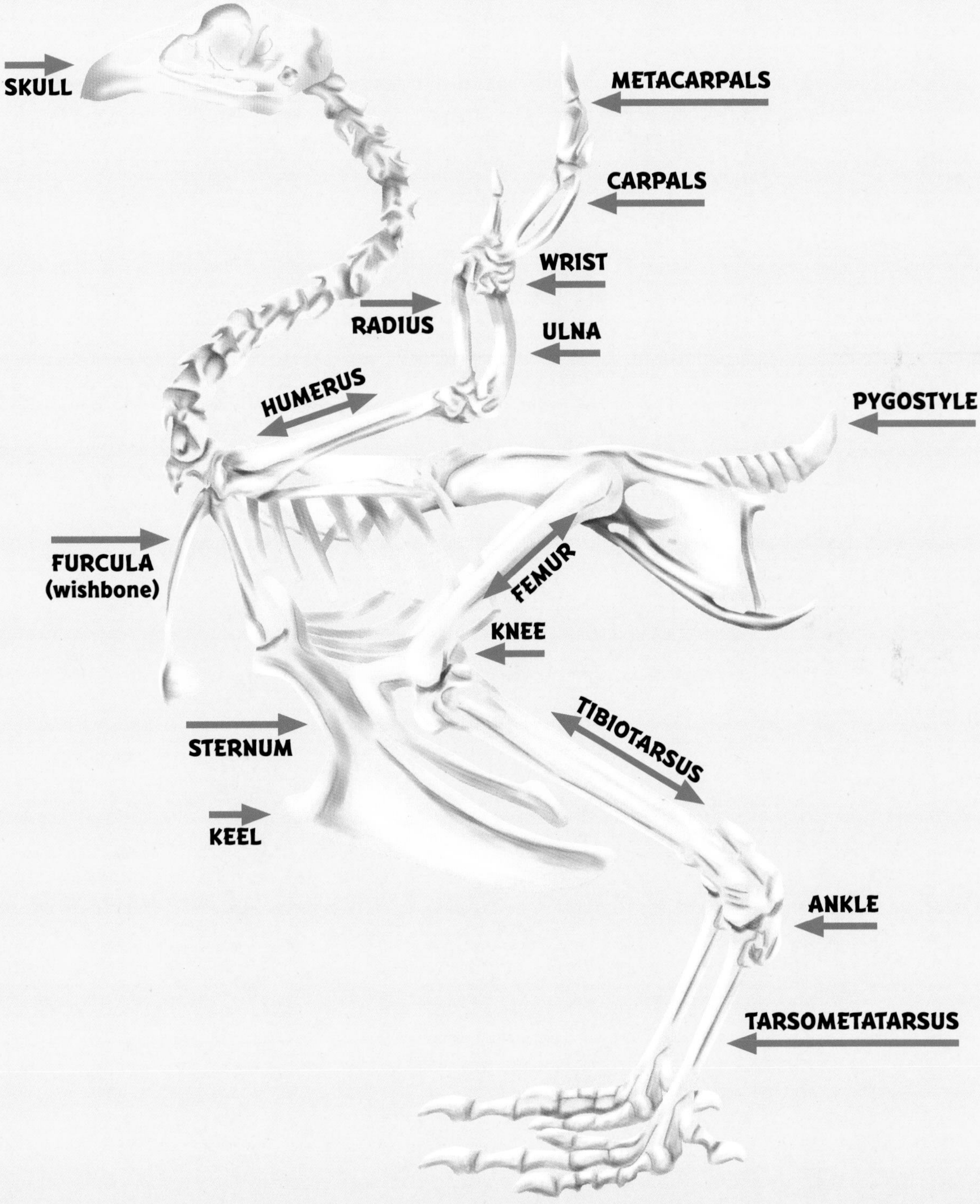

SKULL

METACARPALS

CARPALS

WRIST

RADIUS

ULNA

HUMERUS

PYGOSTYLE

FURCULA
(wishbone)

FEMUR

KNEE

STERNUM

TIBIOTARSUS

KEEL

ANKLE

TARSOMETATARSUS

Bird Sounds

Birds produce a wide variety of sounds, from simple grunts, hisses, and quacks, to some of the most complex, beautiful songs in nature. Birds use their songs to attract mates, and also to tell rivals to stay out of their territories.

Bird songs are even more amazing when you realize that songbirds, such as fairy wrens, larks, sparrows, and finches, have to learn their songs. A young male chaffinch learns its song during the first few months of its life by listening to adult male chaffinches. In some songbirds, such as the rufous-collared sparrow, males may only learn one song, which they sing over and over again. Other birds learn hundreds of songs!

Sound Pictures

Ornithologists who study bird songs don't just think the songs sound beautiful. To bird biologists, songs look beautiful, too! They make drawings called sonograms. The drawings represent sounds, much like sheet music notes. The sonogram below is from a song sparrow. Check out the way a sparrow makes its song by combining many different kinds of sounds.

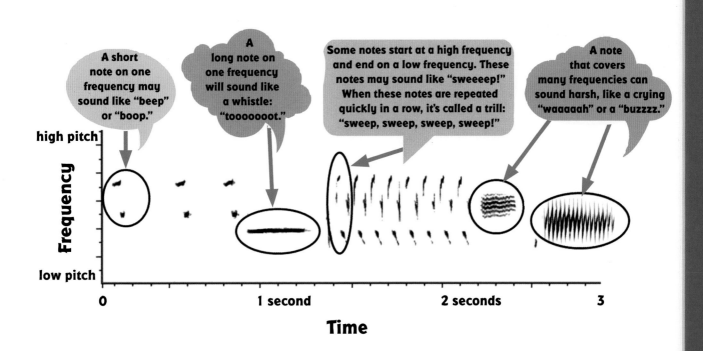

A short note on one frequency may sound like "beep" or "boop."

A long note on one frequency will sound like a whistle: "toooooot."

Some notes start at a high frequency and end on a low frequency. These notes may sound like "sweeeep!" When these notes are repeated quickly in a row, it's called a trill: "sweep, sweep, sweep, sweep!"

A note that covers many frequencies can sound harsh, like a crying "waaaaah" or a "buzzzz."

high pitch

Frequency

low pitch

0   1 second   2 seconds   3

Time

Songs, Voices & Calls

Learning Brains

Ducks, hawks, and storks are born knowing how to make the simple sounds in their quacks, screams, and hisses. Songbirds such as fairy wrens, larks, sparrows, and warblers are different. They have to *learn* their complex and beautiful songs. A young male chaffinch such as this one learns its song during the first few months of its life by listening to nearby adult males.

In some songbirds, such as the rufous-collared sparrow, a male might only learn one song, which it sings over and over again, but a male brown thrasher might learn more than a thousand different songs. No, no, that's not a typo: a male brown thrasher may learn more than *a thousand* songs!

Memory Brains

Not only do songbirds learn the songs they sing, they also learn to recognize the songs that their neighbors sing. In many birds, such as the white-throated sparrow shown below, males can identify all of their next-door neighbors by the unique songs the sparrows sing. When they hear one of their neighbors singing, the birds can relax because they know the singer and where he's supposed to be. But if they hear a stranger in the neighborhood, they go on high alert!

One interesting result of learning songs from your neighborhood is that many birds end up having local accents, just like people. A male song sparrow in Pennsylvania learns a different set of songs than a sparrow in New York. In fact, a New York male might sound so strange that a Pennsylvania female might not like the songs he sings.

WAIT, THERE'S MORE!

In the rare and beautiful North Island saddleback from New Zealand (right), the accents of each small population have become so unique that it's almost as though the birds speak different languages!

Memory Brains

A male hooded warbler can recognize all of his neighbors by their songs. These birds migrate every year, so they only live next to those neighbors for a few months during the summer. You might think they would have to re-learn all their neighbors' songs each year, but their memories are so good that they can even remember their neighbors from the year before.

EASTERN
TOWHEE

WAIT, THERE'S MORE!

Every once in a while, a songbird accidentally learns the wrong song. Eastern towhees sometimes learn the songs of Carolina wrens. You might think that would make it hard for the towhee to communicate with other towhees, but all the neighbors seem to learn the one weird song of their neighbor, and they treat him just like any other towhee.

Mimicking Brains

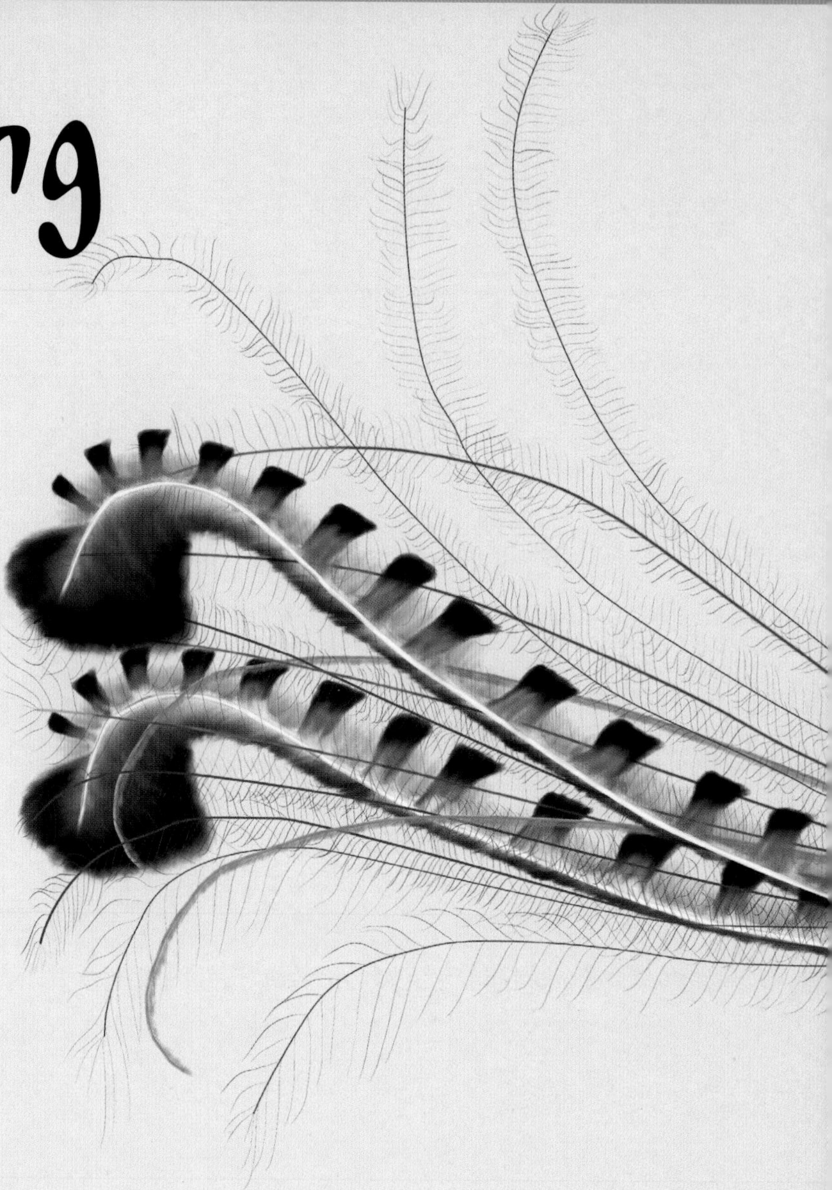

Some other birds are well known for learning the songs of other birds, and these are not just accidents. In North America, male northern mockingbirds may sing the songs of killdeers, northern cardinals, and blue jays. Their songs can also sound like the calls of gray tree frogs or honking car alarms!

MOCKINGBIRD

Another famous bird mimic, the superb lyrebird of Australia, shown here, can imitate a gray shrike thrush bird so well that even the shrikes can be fooled. But why do mimics produce these copycat songs? It's probably not so that they can scare off the other kinds of birds. Even if you're a regular bird-watcher, mimics can fool you. If you listen carefully, though, you will eventually learn to tell the real songs from the imitations. The bird being copied can probably learn the difference, too.

Female Brains

Biologists know a lot about how male birds learn and use songs. Female birds, particularly in tropical parts of the world, learn songs too, and can be spectacular singers. Female streak-backed orioles sing as much or more than males. Female superb fairy wrens use their songs to defend their territories, and they can recognize all of their female neighbors by their songs.

In some species, such as the bay wrens shown here, males and females sing complicated duets. The female starts singing, then the male joins in. Singing pairs alternate notes so perfectly that it almost sounds like one bird singing.

FEMALE
MANAKIN

Double Brains

Unlike most other birds, male long-tailed manakins attract females using teamwork. Two males sing and dance together to catch the female's eye. It can take years of practice for the team to get their performance right. The longer a duo has been together, the more closely their songs match, and matching songs are much more attractive to females. But even after they attract a female, only one male gets to mate. Someday, the other male may inherit the territory. Until then, he has lots of time to practice.

Calling Brains

Birds sing to attract mates, and defend their territories, but those aren't the only things they have to talk about. King penguins breed in huge colonies, which may have one hundred thousand birds. They can recognize their mates by their voices, and chicks can recognize their parents' voices, too. Being able to recognize your family helps make sure that no one gets lost in the crowd.

Talking Brains

Parrots are famous for their ability to learn human language. Parrots do not mimic sounds so that they can talk to people, though. They mimic so that they can talk to their fellow parrots. In the wild, parrots such as the yellow-naped Amazon shown here live in large flocks. These parrots have learned calls that tell which region they are from, and groups that roost together at night share the same calls.

Another parrot, the orange-fronted conure, responds more strongly to the calls of other conures from its local area than to the calls of foreign conures. Brown-throated conures seem to use their calls to attract other conures to foraging areas.

Green-rumped parrotlets learn calls from their parents while they are still chicks in the nest. Each chick learns a unique, individual call, based on the calls that it heard from its parents. Even though each individual's call is unique, the calls of chicks that grow up in the same nest are more similar to one another than they are to the calls of birds from other nests. The parrotlet's calls may be used to recognize individuals, flock mates, or maybe even to call other birds by their name!

Alarm Brains

Black-capped chickadees live in flocks during the winter, and members of a flock will have very similar sounding "chick-a-dee" calls that may help them know who belongs to the flock. They can also use their calls to warn flock members of nearby danger. A big predator, such as a great gray owl, isn't really much of a threat, so the chickadee will call "chick-a-dee." If it spots a more dangerous little saw whet owl, it calls out "chick-a-dee-dee-dee-dee." More *dees* means more danger! When the other chickadees in the flock hear that sound, they don't hide or fly away. Instead, they come rushing in to make sure they know where to find the dangerous owl.

Other species that live near the chickadees understand the chickadee calls, too, and come flying in when a chickadee sounds the alarm. But how do birds such as nuthatches understand chickadee calls? Were they born understanding the calls or did they learn to recognize them? Do nuthatches' alarm calls sound similar? Why do biologists ask so many questions? Interesting questions help scientists design cool experiments!

Tricking Brains

Think about the last time you saw a flock of birds. Did all of the birds look the same? White-winged shrike-tanagers (right) live in flocks with *other* species of birds, such as antshrikes, antwrens, and woodcreepers. These mixed flocks travel the Amazonian rain forest together in big groups, searching for insect prey. Living in these large, mixed groups might help all the birds avoid predators or it might help them find more food. Tanagers give calls that help keep the flocks together.

Tanagers also give alarm calls that alert the flock when they spot a hawk. Sometimes, tanagers give fake alarm calls. When another flock member such as the antwren below finds a large insect, a shrike-tanager gives the hawk alarm. When the antwren dives for cover, the shrike-tanager swoops in and grabs the food!

WAIT, THERE'S MORE!

Superb fairy wrens can understand the alarm calls of one of their forest neighbors, the noisy miner. When a noisy miner gives its alarm call, fairy wrens dive for cover! Not all fairy wrens react this way, though. Wrens that do not share territories with miners do not dive for cover when they hear a miner's alarm call. It seems fairy wrens need to live near miners to learn what their alarm calls mean!

SUPERB FAIRY WREN

Tricking Brains

Fork-tailed drongos use a trick similar to the tanager's trick, combining mimicry and false alarms to steal food from other birds. The drongos can mimic the alarm calls of the pied babbler. When a babbler finds food, the drongo mimics the babbler's alarm call. The frightened babbler flies away when it hears the alarm call, leaving its food behind for the drongo to take!

FORK-TAILED DRONGO

Brown thornbills use false alarms in a different way, to protect their nests. When a pied currawong attacks a little thornbill's nest, as shown here, the thornbill gives an alarm call that makes the currawong think a big hawk is nearby. Currawongs are afraid of hawks and leave quickly when they hear a thornbill's fake alarm.

Building Brains

Many male birds sing or dance to attract mates, but bowerbirds build fancy works of art called bowers instead. Bowers may look like nests, but they are really just a way to impress females. Each species of bowerbird builds a different kind of bower.

Satin bowerbirds build simple stick structures and decorate them with blue objects such as berries, flowers, feathers, or even bottle caps or straws. Females prefer males with fancy, well-built bowers. Why might females like these males better? One idea is that the smartest males build the best bowers, and females like the birds with the best brains.

Male satin bowerbirds do not start displaying bowers until they are seven years old. Young males might need to watch and practice for a long time before they can build a bower good enough to attract a nest mate.

Great Adaptations

Migrating Brains

One of the incredible things birds do is migrate. Many birds take amazing journeys each year, flying across the globe as they move between their summer and their winter homes. Many birds will migrate correctly the first time without anyone showing them the way, but how do they know what direction to go? Birds use many cues, such as the earth's magnetic field or the stars, as their compass.

Young European robins, for example, watch the stars in the night sky and use them to set the compass that guides their migration. Other birds, such as these whooping cranes, learn which way to go from older birds who show the way. After young cranes have made the trip once, they can remember which way and how far to go. They will make the trip every year, flying thousands of miles and returning to almost the exact same places each summer and winter.

Migrating Brains

While some birds make the same migration trip to the same place year after year, other species travel to different places.

Banded stilts live in Australia, where they spend a lot of time on the coast, but they breed in salty lakes, far away in the inland deserts. This lifestyle is tricky because the lakes only fill up after it rains, but it doesn't rain in the same place in the desert every year. Somehow, when the rain falls, large numbers of stilts fly hundreds of miles to their breeding grounds. How do they know when it has rained so far away? How do they find their way? Biologists need to study them more before they can answer these questions!

Upside-Down Brains

Some bird nests are just scrapes on the ground or simple platforms of sticks. Other bird nests are very complex and built high off the ground. Some birds may need to learn skills such as tying knots or weaving grass to make a good nest.

An African bird, the village weaver, builds an amazing nest that's much like a woven basket of grass. The nest hangs from the end of a tree branch, and has an entrance on the bottom. Weaving and knot tying is hard work, but male weaver birds get better as they get older and practice more. After males build nests from green grass or palm leaves, they hang upside down from the nest and flutter their wings, trying to get females to notice their nests.

WAIT, THERE'S MORE!
Female village weavers prefer fresh, green nests. If a female does not pick a nest before the grass fades to brown, males have to start all over again.

Nesting Brains

Picking a safe spot for your nest is important, too. Many birds put their nests out on a thin branch, in a hidden spot in a bush, or in a protected hole in a tree. Some clever birds have figured out other ways to make their nests safe.

To make their nests safer, rock wrens collect thin, flat stones, which are easy to stack, and build a rock wall! These wrens build their nests in cavities or crevices in rocks, but they like the nest opening to be small. If they find a good hole, they might add just a few stones. If the crevice is too big, the wrens will collect hundreds of stones and build a pile of rocks, which blocks off the nest entrance until it's the perfect size.

Nesting Brains

Many other birds have found that they can make their nests safe by nesting near security guards! Rufous-naped wrens often nest in the same trees as wasps. Having so many wasps around helps protect the wrens from white-faced capuchin monkeys. Why do wrens need protection from capuchin monkeys? The monkeys will eat unprotected eggs!

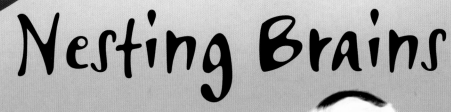

WAIT, THERE'S MORE!
The yellow-rumped cacique and red-cheeked cordon bleu finch also place their nests near the nests of stinging wasps.

Tool Brains

Finding food is another tough job for birds, and they use their brains to make the work easier. The amazing New Caledonian crow actually makes tools to catch insects!

To make one tool, they rip off the edge of a Pandanus tree leaf, and shape the leaf into a thinner strip or a jagged piece with their beaks. They use this tool to pry grubs out of holes in trees. These crows can also make stick tools with hooks from another kind of tree. If the crows make a tool they really like, they may carry it from place to place.

Fishing Brains

Striated herons also use tools, but they use them to catch fish instead of insects! To catch fish, they first collect an object such as a feather or a flower. Then, they drop the object on the surface of the water. When small fish come to investigate the lure, the herons snap them up. Not every striated heron fishes this way, but herons around the world have been seen using lures. Does each striated heron invent bait fishing by itself? Do they learn the trick from other herons? Biologists don't really know the answer . . . yet.

Hunting Brains

Burrowing owls live in underground holes. To find food, these small owls use a trick that's a little like fishing. First, they collect bait. Then, they use the bait to catch prey!

What kind of bait do burrowing owls use? The owls collect animal dung and droppings for bait. Dung beetles eat the feces of other animals, so they are attracted to the dung that the owls collect. The dung beetles think they have found some tasty dung to eat, but they end up being eaten instead.

Feeding Brains

Sometimes, animals find more food than they can eat all at once. What should they do then? Many birds store food for later, but the Clark's nutcracker might be the best at hiding food and remembering where to find it. A single Clark's nutcracker might collect twenty thousand pine seeds and bury them in spots scattered all over its forest home. Then, months later, it can remember where it hid its cache — or, at least, where it hid *most* of them. The seeds it forgets may end up growing into a whole forest of pine trees!

Memory Brains

If you're trying to save food for later, it's important to make sure that someone else doesn't find your buried food first. Steller's jays store food by burying it just below the ground, and they worry all the time that another jay might be watching. If a jay finds a nice peanut at a bird feeder when it's alone, it may store the nut in the ground within a meter of the bird feeder. If only its mate is watching, the jay may fly off and hide the peanut a little farther away. But if a neighbor is watching, then the jay flies even farther away before burying its treasure.

Rufous hummingbirds use their excellent memories to help them find food. As they zip around their territories, drinking nectar from flower after flower, they remember where the best flowers are, and when they last visited them. These memories help them visit the best flowers again when the flowers have re-filled with nectar.

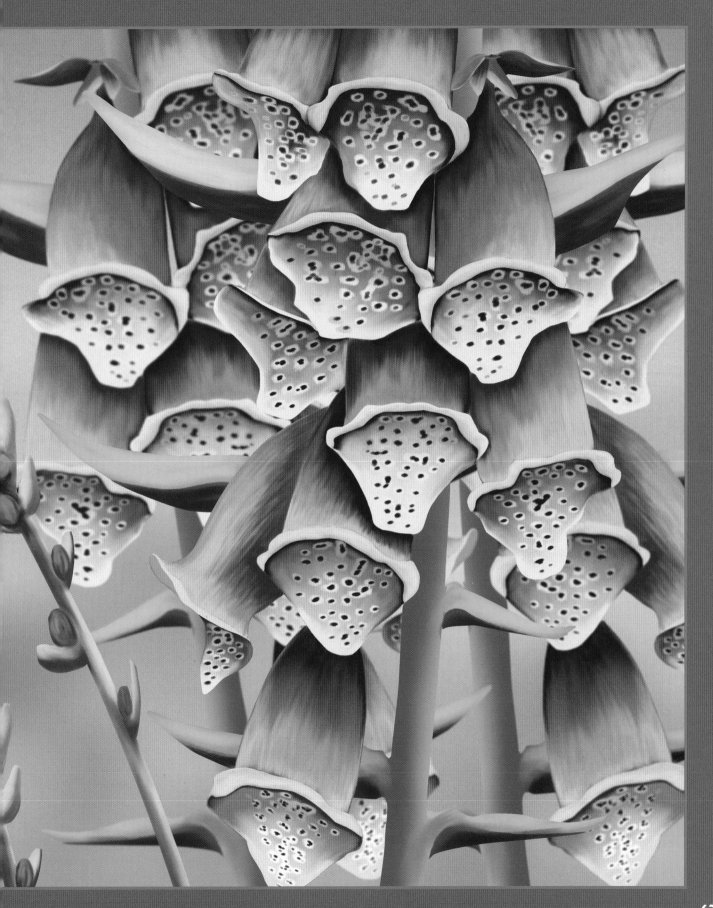

Foraging Brains

Red-knobbed hornbills specialize in figs. In a large rain forest, it's hard to know where to find a tree with these ripe fruits. Somehow the hornbills manage, though. Biologists have noticed that when hornbills find a tree with ripe figs, they often find hornbills feeding. When the hornbills finish eating a tree's figs, they move on to the next fruiting tree, even if that next tree is twenty miles away.

How do hornbills find these trees? Can they spot ripe figs from far away? Do they look for other fig-eating animals and follow them? Do they fly randomly around the forest until they find them? Maybe they remember the locations of good trees from year to year? There's a lot to learn, and biologists love these types of mysteries!

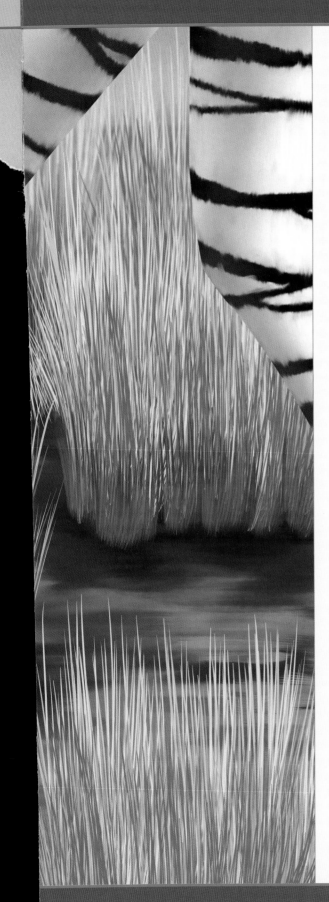

Changing Brains

Birds use their brains to help them survive in their complex environments in so many ways, but being smart can also help birds survive when the world around them changes. People change the world quickly, and being clever can help birds adapt to new problems and take advantage of new opportunities.

Cattle egrets, for example, usually feed around large grazing mammals. In Africa, they often follow zebras, water buffaloes, and rhinoceroses, feeding on small animals such as insects and frogs that the mammals stir up. Cattle egrets earned their common name because they can often be seen feeding around livestock. This behavior has allowed them to spread their range to most places where humans raise cattle. Cattle egrets don't even need cattle to be successful, though. They are just as happy to follow around tractors! All they need is something large moving through the grass and it doesn't matter if it's a wild animal, a domestic animal, or a machine.

Changing Brains

Birds that live in cities have more chances to learn new ways to find food. Many birds around the world take advantage of the food people provide at bird feeders. Monk parakeets (right) have been introduced to many new parts of the world. They can even survive cold northern winters thanks to bird feeders.

The Eurasian blackcap has changed its migration patterns over the last few decades, with more and more birds spending the winter in Britain rather than migrating to the warmer Mediterranean. The food supplied at garden bird feeders may be the key that allows them to survive.

Other birds such as crows, vultures, gulls, and the Australian white ibis find food in human garbage.

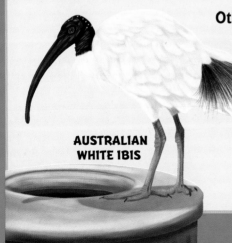

AUSTRALIAN WHITE IBIS

T

Why compete with other animals for food when you can take it from humans instead? Bullfinches in Barbados tear open sugar packets that they can find on the tables in neighborhood restaurants. Ninety miles (145 k) away, on the island of St. Lucia, the closely related Lesser Antillean bullfinches have figured out the same trick.

BANANAQUIT

Bananaquit birds have also been seen eating from sugar packets, but they don't seem to tear sugar packets open themselves. Instead, they can only benefit from the work of the bullfinches. Even on the islands where the sugar thieves are found, it seems that only a few individual bullfinches have learned how to tear open the packets.

A similar story has been seen in keas in New Zealand. Like many parrots, keas are intelligent and curious, and they like to investigate anything they can get their beaks on. In some areas, keas have learned how to open garbage bins to get at food scraps inside. Careful study has shown that only a few keas have actually learned how to open the bins, but many birds in the flock will take food from the bins once they are open. Why is it that only some individuals figure out these tricks?

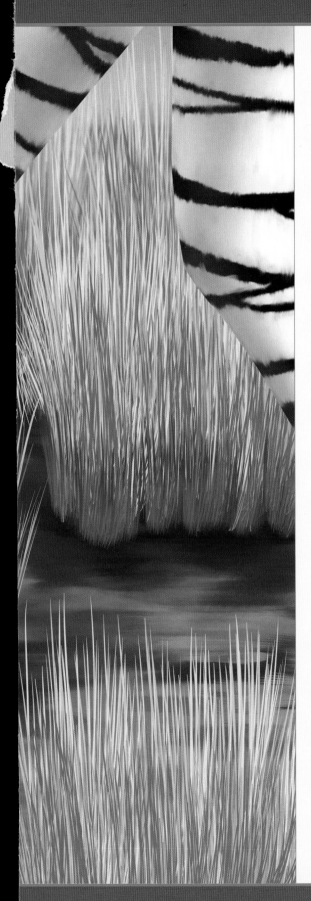

Changing Brains

Birds use their brains to help them survive in their complex environments in so many ways, but being smart can also help birds survive when the world around them changes. People change the world quickly, and being clever can help birds adapt to new problems and take advantage of new opportunities.

Cattle egrets, for example, usually feed around large grazing mammals. In Africa, they often follow zebras, water buffaloes, and rhinoceroses, feeding on small animals such as insects and frogs that the mammals stir up. Cattle egrets earned their common name because they can often be seen feeding around livestock. This behavior has allowed them to spread their range to most places where humans raise cattle. Cattle egrets don't even need cattle to be successful, though. They are just as happy to follow around tractors! All they need is something large moving through the grass and it doesn't matter if it's a wild animal, a domestic animal, or a machine.

Changing Brains

Birds that live in cities have more chances to learn new ways to find food. Many birds around the world take advantage of the food people provide at bird feeders. Monk parakeets (right) have been introduced to many new parts of the world. They can even survive cold northern winters thanks to bird feeders.

The Eurasian blackcap has changed its migration patterns over the last few decades, with more and more birds spending the winter in Britain rather than migrating to the warmer Mediterranean. The food supplied at garden bird feeders may be the key that allows them to survive.

Other birds such as crows, vultures, gulls, and the Australian white ibis find food in human garbage.

AUSTRALIAN WHITE IBIS

Thieving Brains

Why compete with other animals for food when you can take it from humans instead? Bullfinches in Barbados tear open sugar packets that they can find on the tables in neighborhood restaurants. Ninety miles (145 k) away, on the island of St. Lucia, the closely related Lesser Antillean bullfinches have figured out the same trick.

BANANAQUIT

Bananaquit birds have also been seen eating from sugar packets, but they don't seem to tear sugar packets open themselves. Instead, they can only benefit from the work of the bullfinches. Even on the islands where the sugar thieves are found, it seems that only a few individual bullfinches have learned how to tear open the packets.

A similar story has been seen in keas in New Zealand. Like many parrots, keas are intelligent and curious, and they like to investigate anything they can get their beaks on. In some areas, keas have learned how to open garbage bins to get at food scraps inside. Careful study has shown that only a few keas have actually learned how to open the bins, but many birds in the flock will take food from the bins once they are open. Why is it that only some individuals figure out these tricks?

City Brains

If you're a bird living near humans, it may be important not to be too afraid of them, or else you'd be constantly diving into bushes to hide. Many birds, such as the grey heron, live both in cities and out in the countryside.

City birds allow humans to get much closer before they fly away. In some cities, such as Amsterdam, grey herons have become as common as pigeons. But why do urban birds allow humans to get closer? Have they learned not to be afraid of people? Is being fearless a trait birds pass on to their offspring? It's probably a bit of both.

If birds learn to be unafraid of humans, that's only because most of the time, people don't hurt them. However, several species of birds, such as northern mockingbirds, American crows, and black-billed magpies, can *learn* that humans can be a threat. They can also learn to recognize individual humans! Scientists studying black-billed magpies in Korea found that magpies would approach and scold researchers who had climbed up to their nests, but would either fly away from or completely ignore anyone else.

Featured Birds

Glossary

ADAPTATION: A change in an animal's behavior or anatomy that allows it to compete better

BREED: To reproduce

ECOSYSTEM: A community of organisms and the environment where they live

EGG: The female reproductive cell; a fertilized bird egg is called an embryo and can grow into a chick.

FLOCK: A group of birds that spend time together

FORAGE: To search for food

FREQUENCY: The pitch of a sound

HABITAT: The home for an organism or a group of organisms

INVERTEBRATE: An animal that does not have a backbone such as an insect or an earthworm

MIGRATION: An animal's movement from one place to another

NEST: A structure or a shelter used to hold and incubate eggs

ORNITHOLOGIST: A scientist who studies bird behavior, evolution, morphology, and/or physiology

PREDATOR: An animal searching for other animals to eat

PREY: An animal eaten by other animals

RUFOUS: A reddish or reddish-brown color

SIGNAL: Information shared by one organism with another

SONOGRAM: A drawing that shows the frequency and volume over time of a sound or song

SPECIES: A group of organisms that live together in the wild and produce fertile offspring

TERRITORY: An area that a bird or other organism lives in and defends

VERTEBRATE: An animal that has a backbone such as a bird, fish, or mammal

Explore More

CHECK OUT the following websites to learn more about birds and their habitats.
   allaboutbirds.org
   birdlife.org
   ebird.org

Research

To research this book, I drew on information I learned as a student, my own experiences studying birds in the wild, and reading the research of hundreds of other bird biologists.

Index